NOTHING HAPPENED

That's history for you in Old Town—
what's left is where nothing happened.

Nothing Happened

Poems by W. Perry Epes

THE WORD WORKS
Hilary Tham Capital Collection
WASHINGTON, D.C.

The WORD WORKS
PO Box 42164
Washington, DC 20015
editor@wordworksdc.com

Cover art: "American Hitting the Beaches, Greece, 1981." Photo by Steven
                  White. Used by permission.
Frontispiece photo from *Historic Alexandria, Virginia Street by Street*, copyright
                  © 1976 by Historic Alexandria Foundation. Used by permission.
Author photo by Will Mebane.
Book design by Janice Olson.
Printed in the United States by Lightning Source, Inc.

Library of Congress Control Number: 2009936390
International Standard Book Number: 978-0-915380-75-6

ACKNOWLEDGEMENTS

The following poems first appeared (some in slightly different versions) in the following publications: "Coole Park, 1965," *Plume & Sword*; "New Mother" (as "Mother Merrill"), *Negative Capability* and *Anthology of Magazine Verse & Yearbook of American Poetry*; "Visiting Hours" and "Civilian, Late Twentieth Century," *Windfall*; "Radix Malorum," *Escarpments*; "Americans Hit the Beaches," *Woodberry Forest Oracle*; "More Matter with Less Art," *GW Forum* (George Washington University); "The One Who Goes Finds Life," "Tidewater," and "In Cornwall, before Tupping Time," *Phoebe*; "Going to Save the Woods on Fire," *Innisfree*. "Black Fire" appears in *Cabin Fever*, the Word Works anthology of poets who have read in the Joaquin Miller Cabin Series.

To my wife Gail,
admiranda

There is a town near Washington called Alexandria.
My father always talked of going to visit some distant
relations there.
— Lawrence Durrell, *The Alexandria Quartet*

CONTENTS

CIVILIAN, LATE TWENTIETH CENTURY

for Bill Hannum

There's no front line, no rear.
I'll be crouched beside a pocked wall
when gusts of wind assail,
rudely refurling my umbrella,
snatching it up like a dress
above my bared head,
and there I'll be, shucked.

PAST IMPERFECT

As if long prepared for this, as if courageous,
bid her farewell, the Alexandria that is leaving.
                                        —C. P. Cavafy

HISTORY IN OLD TOWN

408 South Lee Street

I

Into the path of our walking tour,
out of this very same fanlit door
where Mother once cradled her newborns home
in the Hepplewhite bureau drawer

a stranger bursts. Her solid wailing
skirls through today like a siren,
drowning the peal of her baby's last bawling—
still as a doll in her baling

arms now. Strung, unstrung, a man shoots past her,
fumbles his keys at the Volvo door.
What can we do?
            Keep out of the way
and remember all that's happened here.

II

Their car horn blares and dies away
through the next block, and the next.

We turn back, and the house looks smaller.
Air conditioning blocks that window
where we had a wood-framed screen
held in by the weight of the sash.
These fixtures come and go with the people.

Quaintly the crooked chimney
soars, still proudly bent
among so many gentrified fronts
with polished plaques of fire brigades
that haven't responded in more than a hundred years.

That's history for you in Old Town—
what's left is where nothing happened.

III

I was six. A workman hanging
our new front gate on its hinges
warned us: "Have it swing out.

Only fools rush in, it's true,
but everyone's got to leave in a hurry
sometime."

IV

Four when I had my tonsils out
and overdosed on penicillin.
Summer locusts swelled in my room,
shook the bed with their chirring.

Still, when I close my eyes,
the one that chased me down the hall
is waist-high. I open again
so nothing will happen.

The part I never saw:
my father leaping from sleep
to hold me before I could claw the screen
and plunge from that window over the door.

One day I'll have a child to lose
and something brave to do.

V

"He changed." My sister knows.

"Mummy had bleeding, when you were born,
from where they'd sewn her up.
Daddy thought he might faint.
She seized his wrist and ordered him
not to. That's when he changed."

Three years later my sister came
with her own self-hurting temper,
      and he was ready
to spring down a flight of stairs
and snatch away the broken glass
in the time it took her to drop her bottle
and reach down to pick up a shard
and decide to bite down on it.
     "Sometimes I wish
he'd gone ahead and let me."
     "Nonsense," I say.

BERKELEY SPRINGS, 1886

In memoriam Nathaniel Beverley Tucker *(1820-1890)*

Full-dress summer evenings.
Sparks and belles in the promenades;
much doffing to gouty elders.
Outside a cottage creaking with offspring,
Grandfather pants in the yard.

Big jolly old man, who bantered with Mr. Cleveland
the night before the inaugural:
"What you can do for me, Grover,
is clap your hand on my shoulder tomorrow
in front of all those people, and call me Bev."

Bev's children's children remember this year
for the whooping cough he caught from them.
Apart in the airless twilight,
there's Grandfather grasping each gatepost
and the whole length of the picket fence shaking.

THE BISHOP ENCOUNTERS THE TWENTIETH CENTURY

In memoriam Beverley Dandridge Tucker *(1846-1930)*
Virginia Beach, 1927

I

Sunday morning on the boardwalk.
Portly gent in a Panama hat
is marching six short blocks to Galilee
Chapel, vestments draped on his arm,
pinafored granddaughter in tow.
He's touching up his sermon
on Robert E. Lee, the Christian soldier.

Stops short, and glances down
where supine bathers cure in the sun

    like bright leaf edges.
    And to what end? Going up in the smoke
    of lust stripped bare?

He raps his cane, and the railing rings
six blocks each way.

    "Rise up, good people! Come all to church!
    You'll feel so much happier!"

    Heads pop up.
From here and there a laugh drifts back.

    My mother, the little pinafored girl
    who played solitaire
    in the vesting room
    during that sermon,
    is still embarrassed.

II

From the sermon

By faith Moses, when he was come to years, refused
to be called the son of Pharaoh's daughter, choosing
rather to suffer afflictions with the people of God...
                    —Heb. 11:24-25

In the gorgeous palace of the Pharaohs, Moses stood in the presence of a temptation like to that when the Son of Man was shown all the kingdoms of the world and the glory thereof.

In the making of this decision, we find the keynote to the character of Lee. He was offered command of the forces of a great and powerful nation. On the other hand was all that sacrifice could mean, the espousal of a doubtful cause, the loss of property and of home, hardships for his loved ones and himself.

This is the true spirit of the Christian, the readiness to renounce, the willingness to endure, for righteousness' sake. The choice that Moses made, the choice that Lee made, the choice that you and I make, is to be determined by faith in the living God.

I saw him once in the Sunday-School room at a Lenten service at seven in the morning. Old Traveller was hitched to the telegraph pole outside. He who led the armies of the Confederacy was humbly bowed in prayer. He had started, at break of day, from his headquarters and had ridden more than ten miles to seek guidance and strength in the House of God.

Oh, my friends, it is a great privilege which the name and memory of Robert E. Lee bring to us. We can hold him up to those who come after us, not so much for what he did as for what he was.

                    —*Tales of the Tuckers, 1942*

III

From the vesting room, my mother heard
only his flushed aside
on sparking Miss Mary Triplett,
belle-to-be of the Sulphur Springs,
in Richmond, after the war.
One Sunday
on the front porch on Franklin Street,
when General Lee strolled by
in his greatcoat with the buttons cut off,
just like the men's, he bent to kiss
his pretty young cousin
and winked at the rapt young man.
"Now don't you wish, Mr. Tucker,
that you could do that too?"

IV

In the other '60s, my mother
is giving her final chapel talk
as head of a Quaker school,
greening the young
with the bishop's simple believing:

"I was eight and he eighty-two
the summer I lived at the Beach.
We always swam before breakfast.
He'd lean on his cane in the surf,
roly-poly with thick white hair
and a wide-striped woolen bathing suit
sagging to the knees.

One morning a sudden backwash
swept us out. I grabbed for his cane;
my weight, it turned out, righted him.
Spluttering back, we flopped on the beach.
To cousins, uncles, and aunts
at breakfast, he gravely announced
that I had saved his life that day,
and he made them all stop laughing."

THE LAST CRUISE OF THE HERMANN FALK

In memoriam W. Perry Epes *(1913-1962)*
   Newport News, 1923

I

Swamped in silt where tidefall stains the pier,
one lifeboat left from a German freighter
impounded at Newport News, then broken up
and sold for scrap.
                        My father,
        living out as an only child
        his bad boy's story (told and told
        for me to cheer, and learn some things),
inveigles school-cowed cousins into hooky.
Slinging down their satchels of Latin and Shakespeare,
straggling down to the water's edge,
they clump around his whooped eureka—
traces of buried gunwales on the beach!
He paws at the sand to clear some freeboard,
brushes free a few letters—F, A, L . . .
They jump in to help him bail,
digging all day, shirtless. Even Cousin Lewis
desists
        from penning yet another play
with himself as king, and heaves ho
to chock the hull with stray planks and crabpots—
makeshift ways
where Cousin Horace will sweat in the sun,
patching the keel with tar paper.
        Three more days
my father plots courses on tattered charts
from a back room of the tackle shop,
wishing up storms they'll have to brave—
new tossings on shallow waters.

           All set for the maiden voyage
on a summer weekday (paters safely
off to work).
      Scrubbed like a steward,
"First Mate" Horace hands them in,
the spinster cousins and baby sisters,
mothers fussing, deaf old great-aunt Agnes—

layers them in
around and over the wicker hampers
packed with jellies, ham and beaten biscuits,
chicken and deviled eggs (no jerky),
silver, and crockery chinked with linen
for the picnic spread at Buckroe Beach.

"Commodore" Perry stays aft, in needed space
for handling the tiller and trimming the main.

      (a gaff rig always looks broken-masted,
      hung like a kite by tension on the sheet)

Old Agnes leans her trumpet
blankly, into the wind,
can't hear his "Ready:
About!"
      but has no weight to bother shifting.

And "Lord" Lewis, self-styled "concierge,"
who has not forgot
his tome of best-loved poems,
will render some Browning
      just as they
      "gain the cove with pushing prow
      and quench its speed i' the slushy sand."

II

Return

In irons,
       down in the water.
My father sends Horace forward
to step on seepage by the foot of the mast.
Soon it's over his shoe. Much headway
must have shorn a patch.

       Babies sleep on.

Aunt Agnes smiles and nods.
Lewis offers to sing familiar *lieder*,
but matrons frown and tuck their hems up,
wondering how they'll face their tired husbands
at the end of this storied day

       which I'll hear about from my lawyer dad
       on a landward ride
       to Buckroe's tacky amusement park,
       where I'll chicken out at the roller coaster
       and stuff my mouth with cotton candy.
       He'll scowl

       when I ask what letters he won
       in team sports at school.

None!
but we knew real danger on trackless waters.

Yeah, Dad. What went down?

In the end, nothing.

Horace, in the dead calm, mans the oars
while Lewis coxes, off and on.
My father,

who'll die before he can trust me
with a boat,

stays steady at the helm.
They beach her again at Buckroe, for good,
and everyone rides the trolley back home.

Lord Jim on the Eastern Shore

(1961)

I

White on black   on black   on black
      white black   white black—
the center line blinks past
      so sad and relaxed
in my sister's 7th-grade poem
about driving home down Route 13
      our summer flights
from ex-pat Philadelphia.

She won a prize
for catching the skip-rope beats
      of little black girls,
      dark in mottled shade
at the tamped edges of the fruit stand clearing
where we pulled over,
      swirling dust.

She talked to them,
      could talk to them,
swing ropes with them,
      hop in, hop out
      jumping off the train
      at pretty girl station
and gently prize open their clenched grins
to loose their songs

while I stood firm at the counter, seeing to it
      change was made correctly.

Her closing line:
      My brother is Lord Jim.

II

Sulking back to school up Route 13
on Trailways, trying to turn at least one page
of my 9th-grade summer reading—
      Conrad, with whom
my father wrestled long.
He knew this "mental fight" would bless me, too,
and read me the paper he wrote in college:
"If ever you've tried to start a car on a cold morning,
when the engine sputters, chokes, flares again,
backfires maybe, and finally roars to life,
      then you have some idea
      of the narrative pace of *Lord Jim*."
I could stall all August, and make him smile—
      "It just ain't roared to life yet, Dad!"—
and wheedle an extra week at the beach
      if I promised to finish.

     Now, on the bus,
      hardly a page between stops—
      Little Creek, Kiptopeke, Eastville—
      Boy! this is a local!
      The vinyl head rest
feels oily. Better not fall asleep.
Drool on the page. That girl across the aisle,
pretty redhead, will I dare to speak to her,
      the only other white passenger?

Nassawaddox, Exmore—
      "Shitfire!" from up front,
and I turn back through dense prose
to see if the *Patna* hit something.
      Why are we coasting? Why is the driver

pumping the brake and easing the wheel
to slow the bus with swerves?
"Sweet Jesus, we ain't gonna make this!"

One last swerve
to plant the right front corner of the chassis
smack in the bed of the cantaloupe truck
        that turned too slow,
and the whole bus shudders like a rack of dishes.

"Whooee! Anyone hurt? Please, folks,
        don't nobody leave the scene."

He shoves back his red cap. "Now these heah
is witness cards." He passes them out
and steps down to jaw with the trooper.
        Off alone,
the bumped black truck farmer,
dusty and crinkled as all his fenders,
down at the moping mouth
with nothing to plead . . .

        I bend to my card.
Your name, address? And who, in your judgment . . .?
Murmurs from the back of the bus. A grizzled uncle
waits on me to heed his proffered card.
"Could you write it, Mister? We ain't got no pencils."
Eight more behind, wide eyes begging me
not to offer to lend them mine.

So I take their names and depositions.
Who's at fault? The Trailways representative
or operator of other vehicle?
 Yassuh. Who? De truck man? Sho'.
Whatever the young gent'man writes down.

I stand up to deliver their cards.
Oh, and the redhead's, too.

So where's she from?
New Jersey. Teaneck. Boyfriend in the Navy.
    "I don't approve
of the way you treat these people down here."

    Oh. I should have refused
    to write for them?

"You never thought of asking my help.
It could be the bus was going too fast."

I quail on the spot, hand to my lips
(Jim's final gesture, I later will read,
when he's shot by the natives he cannot save
from Gentleman Brown the pirate).

OK, OK, she could win the War
    all over again.
I shuffle back to my seat, where a nickel's left
    on the unturned page.

Change, I think. All they could spare.
Or all my services are worth.

An elegy I wrote my father
upset my mother almost as much
as "Lycidas" bothered Dr. Johnson.
There were no shepherds in mine,
but she deplored it
for "shying away from direct statement"
and asked me to consider
what I might have left out.

I know I failed to hammer into rhyme
my father's jaunt in the car
to look at colleges with my older sister
three months before he died.
My mother drove, but on the way home
was stricken with something
and yielded to nausea every few miles
by the side of the road. My sister
had only her permit; my father,
though in and out of hospital beds
for the last six months, took over
and handled the last hundred miles.
How proud he was when they made it home!
We all ran out to greet them,
my younger two sisters and I,
and helped him help my mother to bed.
When the sitter needed a short ride home,
he joked about going the extra mile.

"No, that's not the tone of the story!"
My mother speaks directly. "No, that trip
was purely a nightmare—
tedium, shame of his failing kidneys,
his swollen limbs and bloated face;

people in restaurants looking away,
the motel clerks pretending there were no vacancies.

No matter how they stared,
I couldn't make them see us!
Nor can you."

COMING ABOUT

A pier in summer. The older kids
keep diving as the tide falls.
I sit and watch for my year,
cheer the boys grown taller and taller,
watch one swelling girl.
She climbs back up the ladder,
stands there dripping, pulls her straps up.
I make a place on the bench for her.
She snaps back, in front of all ages:
"I'm not sitting next to you!"
　　At mean low water,
flailing like a flywheel,
Charlie Boy back flops, and bobs up
gagging. Thinks he's swallowed
a jellyfish. She gathers a crowd of us
in a chanting ring on the beach, to help him
puke it up. He doesn't have to,
and she's his, we think, for the rest of the summer.
　　At dead low water, mud flats stretch away
a mile or more, and the riverbed
seethes and stinks like a drained pond.
We slip on sneakers with no laces
to check this bottom we can't see
while swimming or wading, mostly barefoot.
Pay no mind to rusty cans
and broken bottles, oyster shells
that'll pare your toes. Only what moves:
fiddlers scooting with one big claw
upraised, and hard-shell crabs
whose outstretched arms don't welcome us,
and fish like this one, trapped in a pool,
croaker, bloater, toadfish in one,
the kind of trash we cut the line for. Our ring
gathers. I stick a toe out

to nudge it, taunt it; when it lunges
we hear the jaws snap, and we have,
for the next high tide, a warning.
After we've fallen back,
she bends over my foot, like a blacksmith,
and I lean for balance
on her bare shoulder.

Beau was as weird as he was dumb.
Old family name, pronounced "good know"
and spelled, in fact, like "good enough,"
but we'd reverse it to "Bo No-*Goood*"
and laugh at his mannered indignation.
Remedial kid
who'd swallowed a dime when he was little
and talked funny, like Andy Devine.

One day, down by the pool, in the dressing room—
wood stockade around a bare dirt floor,
open to the sky—Beau (short for Mirabeau)
took a dump
because it was too long a way
back up the hill to the can by the cabins.

Another day, toward the end of the noon swim,
I had to go real bad. I asked to be excused
and pranced into the dressing room to change.
Pains shot up my bowels—couldn't wait—
squatted in the corner. Out it came
in one long turd, the biggest I'd ever seen.
Quickly I pulled on shorts and shirt
and ran up the hill to wipe myself.

Camp buzzed all day.
I was off somewhere, at archery or riding,
when they made Hank pick up his mess
again, and carry it out in a napkin.
No one has ever known about this.

Close hauled off Old Point Comfort,
beating to windward all afternoon
till we rounded that drifting crabpot
moored to an empty skiff

and the wind stopped beating back,
and we saw, in the calm, the waterman's head
where he waded, up to his shoulders,
trailing the painter from a loop around his neck.

Going to Save the Woods on Fire

for John Walker

Halfway through the seventh verse of "Pretty Polly,"
just after Willie tells her she's guessed it 'bout right,
for he'd dug on her grave the best part of last night,
Jack Hubert jumps up at the first chance not to listen.
His big shadow gestures sway against the near trees
in campfire glow, reaching toward a pinpoint of light
on the far ridge across the lake, like a shot star
in the woods. "That'll be up Cy Beede's Ledge," he growls,
blaming cigarette butts tossed by weekend guests
the summer people bring up there, on the short hike
to a near overlook, for the cheapest good view.

Jack's time is winter, when the lake will freeze four feet
and he can drive his tractor across, do heavy work
like hauling Calor gas tanks, and not put up with
the filthy rich New Yorkers and Philadelphians
who own these camps. The people I'm working for now,
as summer cook and guide, trekked in one Christmas Eve.
No sooner had they settled in than Jack showed up
with the cold facts: they could leave in twenty minutes
or stay three weeks in the blizzard blowing up.
They staggered out on a tow rope behind his tractor
in blinding swirls of snow. None will hear Jack tell
of wild dogs circling, one child dropping off,
but their own little Polly (for whom I learned the song)
believes to this day in lore of the hounding wolves.

One of us tries a thought: "Could be a campfire, Jack."
But it's still a damn-fool thing in this heat and drought.
We'll have to check it out. I lay aside my guitar,
knowing I can't guard it in the rush we'll be in.
We smother our fire with scoops of sand, not water.
I shove off first with Billy Koop, who lets me row
his Adirondack guide boat, narrow-beamed and fast.

The knack is pulling cross-handed; skinned my knuckles raw
in weeks of practice. Billy's been learning my songs
while showing me how to caulk a keel with oakum—
weird stuff, like hemp rope steeped in tar; you knead it
and pound it into the cracks with wooden mallets.
Now he hums "Pretty Polly," coiled there in the bow
that slits taut water like a point of shears. We cross

a shadow-line where the nearing shore blocks moonlight.
Gliding into this dark stirs dread we've swallowed back
all summer: banshee cries of loons in shore,
then crashing in the bushes—that's no loon
but a yearling cub caught whimpering for its
mother, and she'd be one to miss this time of year.
We'd hoist up and topple the oars, slap them flat
like pistol cracks to warn all nature, "Here we come!"
Tonight, though, we need no noise. From the other guide boat,
off and on, Jack Hubert whoops to beat us across
with rousings. The mountain shadow's solid no more,
pricked by that pinpoint light, reflected, looking bigger.

Follow Me Down
Field Studies in Leadership

I am the Infantry. Follow me!
> —Poem on Wall, Foyer of Infantry Hall, Ft. Benning, Georgia

1
Black Fire

Poring over the contour map
of somewhere out West—slopes of gulches
where leaping flames outrun the deer—
I spot a smudge and smokejump in,
spiraling down through my convex lens
that can swell a campfire ring
to a dark lake, then, nearer,
the lost doe's liquid eye
that swallows me in
without a ripple.

2
A File of Fellow Soldiers

In boot camp, we learned to read
our topo maps to use the terrain
and practiced guiding a file of fellow soldiers
not straight up and over
but all along a contour line
to spare fatigue and grief. "The ease of your men,"
our captain claimed,
"their gratitude for leadership,"
would be, he promised, palpable.
"It might could be
as smooth as pleasing a woman."

Our best at it was Carolina Jim,
a boy from Boone who jollied us all,
even Tangedahl, the stolid Norwegian farm boy

from North Dakota,
whom he nicknamed Tangle-balls
and took along whoring in Columbus.

Me, already married, he largely ignored.
But one morning, next to me
in formation, he muttered
while trying to squeeze a belt end
into its buckle, "Tight,
like the fit last night," and looked up
and took me in with a grin.

The next night we were only men
in the dark, in squads of fours,
orienteering to beat the terrain,
straight over whatever contour
to find set stakes in thickets and gullies.
Carolina Jim, while tracking an azimuth
on the glowing face of the compass,
kept swatting his neck.
From the rear, counting paces,
I called a halt
and offered him my stick of Cutter's.
"God damn, boy! You been hoardin' this stuff."
And he pocketed it.

Seventeen hundred and fifty-eight paces
we'd slogged, I shifting a smooth pebble
from one pants pocket to the other
for every hundred. I got the distance
while he was blowing direction.
Damn if I'd walk
another mile in his prints!

Ranging yards to the left and right,
we finally found the first stake.
I snatched that fuckin' compass face
and marched us off on our next azimuth,
a hundred and eighty-two degrees.

3
Parade Rest

One more thing our captain cried,
tracing his crown with thumb and finger
and flicking away the sweat

while we stood still in the sun
at parade rest, and the sergeant's eyes
popped wide to see me

sneak reaching in the second rank
for my canteen, and then relaxed to a squint
when he saw I saw he saw. I slid it back

to its holster, snug as an unfired gun,
and the captain set his garrison cap
on his gleaming pate, and launched again:

"My good followers!" Pause. Flick. "At sea level
your contour line goes out and around
the whole damn world. You could march forever!"

Oh captain, our captain!
Here in this sump by the sea
that's thick with the oily ports

our fathers shipped from,
tilted down from their pioneer hills
to fight again in the Old World,

we're mustered now
for another forced march the length of the coast
to the next grunts' hellhole.

Mortal footmen can only snicker
at high and mighty bald spots
going on before.

4
Young Men and Fire

God was not in the fire and wind
but a still small voice the foreman heard
when he lit a back-fire
and crouched in that airless space
that the main blaze truly abhorred
and leapt right over. Breath
rushed in behind. The others, trapped
in forgivable panic, heard not
or heeded not his call
and tried to race the blow-up
over the ridge. Two made it. Thirteen
were roasted alongside an eight-point buck,
charred fossil no vulture would touch.

Norman Maclean, a ranger in that forest
when a river ran through it,
much later taught me criticism
at the University of Chicago.

Along with that foreman, he brooded
for the rest of his life
about how to tell this story.

5
Down in the Doe's Eye

*I used to think water was first, but if you listen
carefully you will hear that the words are underneath
the water.*
— Norman Maclean

Beneath our Sahara, earth's burning skin,
aquifers shift and heave.
Fire and water are one.

Millions in lone determination
surge upstream
to penetrate our maiden godhead.

From that still center,
any way out is down or up.

Selves melt in the flowing wall
of birth and after-birth.

Oneness lives on
in the tumble of endless division.

Squad pinned down by small arms fire
behind some wall of flaking stucco
draped in vine tongues

warping the slats of French Colonial jalousies.
Unknown soldier crouches,
feeds his M-16 a clip;

the weapon sweeps in reflex arcs,
describing fields of fire.
Incoming! Incoming! Right damn here!

He cowers down under the window.
His arm, with his gun, flails up
to swat across his shoulder

at every pestering thing.
The muzzle bobs and spits,
the stock convulses for one clip's worth,

and the inner flesh of that house
soaks up bullets.
He slumps against the wall,

flips a bird at the cameraman
jogging over for an interview.
Just then, as he lights up,

an upper hinge gives,
and *finally* the splintered jalousie
swings down and clunks his helmet.

He jumps up and claps his head,
snatches the camera, swings wild arcs.
Our framed world kaleidoscopes,

blacks out.

Americans Hit the Beaches

(in loco parentis, on the Greek isle of Hydra)

This was the day I finally told the Stanley twins apart.
We filed off the cruise boat, fanned out through town,
fending off vendors and guide books, aiming straight as possible
for beaches beyond the basin of the harbor.
Two days of old rock piles in Athens and Mycenae,
and now it's all isles and sun; no more need for awe
at spears and shields and helmets
hammered out upon a time, or buckled on
with no thought that we would travel in coaches
to jog through the museums in shorts and Nikes.
Time now for stripping down to bathing suits,
being ourselves and looking each other over,
filling the lungs with open air, and shouting them empty—
our own music at outdoor dancing on the sand.
    No such beach—where a sign in pidgin
said "This is the place swimming," only a moderate cliff
and piles of surf-lashed rocks. A dip in the sea
meant backing gingerly down one ladder
till one of the Stanleys climbed the cliff unnoticed, and jumped.
We gasped at the plunge and splash, held breaths till the head
    bobbed,
and cheered. The other Stanley matches the feat exactly,
then all the boys, and even one of the girls. Stakes mounting—
Stanleys add twists and gainers, others jump in tandem.
A crowd of tourists gathers, the real draw being
the chance to see a body brained on the rocks.
I ask one Stanley to cool it. He asks for just one more.
I leap on this concession. "All right, but nothing fancy.
Just jump, and wrap it up." But why one more?
As they climb again, I chew me out, rehearsing
the orders I should have given. Their every step
is a station of the cross I have to bear.
You could say they never were meant to live—
conception "complete surprise"; three pounds each at birth;

incubated brawn, motherlove hovering for years.
And I, *in loco*, know nothing of hatching youth
but cracking shells on rocks, like gulls with oysters.

They're up, radiant in height. What's left but prayer?
the last resort of dads. They jump,
arms locked and all for one, with nothing fancy—
John on the left, and Wade on the right. My burden
melts to a thick joy you could cut with a knife
for sharing 'round. Even before the double splash
I believe in their last jump: one more just for me
so I can learn to bear these pangs
for the length of each plunge in the wine-dark sea.

In Cornwall, before Tupping Time

Even now, now, very now, an old black ram
Is tupping your white ewe.   —Othello

Schoolgirl, ten. Three years ago her Mum and Dad
moved down from Oxfordshire,
from riding school and desk job, to farm.
Mud to the sills, boot jack on the doorstep
for pulling off your mucky green wellies.
Healthy barn stink gently floats everywhere.

"What do you learn in America?"
Her first question becomes her refrain
as she tours us round the coops and cowshed,
scolds a cockerel by name, silly boy!
for hopping up on the table
in the midst of cream tea in the garden.

After tea, Sir Alec calls—
a canvass, he says, for the local Tories
but really to see his mare, gone lame
from a nasty kick and a bite on the withers,
put to grass with these milder sheep.
"Oh my, that's looking prouder," he says,

and I can follow, recalling
how Penn Warren first wrote *All the King's Men*
as a play called *Proud Flesh.* And the sheep,
pail-fed and tame, come boiling over the hill
to nuzzle our palms and bleat for praise.
But it's scolding again, for Lucy,

that woolly ewe, has rolled in mud
and is smeared as ever in tupping time!
Sir Alec darts me a glance. "You know
what that means?" Oh yes, from teaching Shakespeare.
Ah, and he's freed to tell his joke
about Sunday School, and the parable

of 99 sheep and why the shepherd cared so
for one stray lamb. "Because," the plough boys jeered,
"because it were the tup!" Our schoolgirl laughs.
One ram, you see, can service the whole flock.
We chain a smear on his neck,
like a big lipstick, to leave his mark

on each ewe he's mounted. "In America
do you study nature in the schools?"
In a fashion, yes. My very first class,
all boys with one black student, perked right up
at tupping Desdemona. Yes, I told them,
thank your teacher who tells you what you've learned
about everything you know already.

OUR ALEXANDRIA

The Protestant Episcopal Theological Seminary in Virginia,
founded 1823

One of my wife's classmates at the Seminary,
from Taiwan, interrupted a lecture once
to ask if the 3rd century church father,
Clement of Alexandria, was from here
in Virginia. Instead of laughing
the professor wondered, Is there any way
we could make this true?
There is an old iconic tradition
of sacred conversation,
Abraham and Moses, Peter and St. Paul
all gathered around a table with Jesus . . .

Well, the town fathers already tried
with the George Washington Masonic Memorial,
built 1932, supposedly an exact replica
of Alexander the Great's lighthouse,
a wonder of the ancient world
that collapsed in 54 A.D.
This vague attribution lives on,
but George's temple is still not beautiful.

When you go in, the remnant old Masons
who give the tours are most uncertain
about mystical rites, cannot explain
the mural of the *hajj* to Mecca
or why they wear fezzes for Shriners' parades
in their miniature cars.

Nor is the Seminary's own tower
(1859, proto-Victorian Italianate,
often mistaken for pagoda-style)
at all beautiful—grotesque, even,
to low-church sensibilities
with their furtive pride in stark simplicity.

Not truly ugly, Aspinwall,
just bold, immediately incongruous
in this politely brooding place
still framing its Reconstruction story,
stubbornly self-effacing.

Once a visiting English bishop
asked how the tower was funded.
With grateful contributions, it is said,
for missionary work in China.
"Well," the bishop quipped, strolling on
with his arms behind his back,
"the Chinese certainly got their revenge."

THE ONE WHO GOES

I would say she was memory,
and we were restored by
the radiance of her illusion,
her consummate attention to detail.
    —Mark Doty, *My Alexandria*

HIS ONLY MOTHER

"How do I know you're my only mom?"
(his first recorded question). She just laughed.
Expecting again, she was sure he meant
Am I still your only boy?

And no one expected his next move
when a sister came. "You jammed on
your Sunday cap, and marched up Quaker Lane
to Uncle Bland's" (who had no kids at all).

He's laughed along, but never quite remembered
meaning all that. While Mother taught poise
at hearts and bridge and other games
of chance and social bidding,

he'd ache to hear this story over,
reaching back to his quiver of doubts
to shoot the moon, and prick her
into telling the end. "You slunk straight home.

I cooked up your favorite treat
(a lemon meringue) and set it to cool.
You stomped right into the kitchen
and slopped that pie in the garbage pail."

CALLY

I never heard your last name,
never dreamed I needed it. "Cally!" I'd say,
and climb in your lap
to feel you sing or hear your heart beat.
Never met your husband, or the "troublous" son
you sighed and clucked your tongue over
while Mother shook her head politely.

You trekked north with us to Pennsylvania
in the front seat of the '41 Buick.
Mother drove, while you leaned over the seatback
to talk with us
in the pit for toys and kids and pets
where the back seat was ripped out.
You stayed on for two whole weeks—
"forever" enough
for us kids to agree to the move.

My mother shakes her head.
"Don't you forget how hurt Cally was
that time she buckled your baby shoes
and you kicked her in the stomach. Just a reflex,
but she never trusted you again,
even knowing you were too little to mean it."

I do remember, in Pennsylvania,
Cally taught me to tie my Buster Browns.
Not that everyone else didn't try.
My daddy explained it, over and over.
Mother showed me, face to face,
but only Cally would kneel down over my shoulder
(splash of bay rum, cool mint breath on my cheek)
and trace my hands through the bows till I saw.

Rixey's Rage

What if his students saw him
smack himself in the head ten times
for not bringing the right change
to the Xerox machine?

This heat's inherited. His father's white star rage
threw its flame light years.

And what if his mother had seen
his father hurl the sickle down
that bounced along the garage floor
between him and Rixey, who'd only wanted
to keep his first paid job
cutting weeds in a vacant lot
instead of joining the family's search
for their dog that ran off
from a picnic in Valley Forge Park?

She only heard her husband roaring
till Rixey wet his pants:
"If this family were an engine,
you'd be pouring sand in the sump!"

His wife asks Rixey, "How did that *feel*?"
"Ashamed for wanting. My father was right,
but I never got to *say* even that."

That evening, his mother told Rixey
to steer a careful course
this side of provoking his dad.
"You kept asking, asking—
just like the time you taunted him
about sports he never played."
She had enough to do to keep his temper

from spiking his blood pressure
to levels of stroke or heart attack.

Now Rixey—father dead, no son of his own
to burn—plays only a daylight glare
on the bent heads of his students.

VISITING HOURS

I drive up in March rain
to the Children's Rehab Center
and take a long time backing and filling,
make up a final checklist:
lights, wipers, brake, ignition.
The sidewalk between me and the truth
gets shorter with each step.
Through swinging glass doors,
no nurse at reception
to tell me that visiting hours
are over. Halfway down the corridor
one nods in passing:
Peter is three doors to the left.

    Just now he's quiet. I stand at the foot of the bed,
hands folded and wanting
a doffed hat to hold.
I lean to block the overhead glare.
My eyes and Peter's lock
in a stare not utterly blank
and not entirely afraid.
A spasm seizes this sixth-grade soccer star
who fell into a diabetic coma
and woke up three months later
screaming, convulsive—
jerks up the knees
to meet with and jam the fists
into mouth wide-opened, almost unhinged,
and all the might of the scream
is strangled by his
whole body's
isometric.

    The nurse is there to unfold him
and pull those fists from the lip
where the teeth have almost cut through.

I have to wonder why this had to happen,
am even about to ask her
when the spasm starts over. I'm asked instead
if I'd like to help this time.
While she unbends the knees,
I lean my weight to keep the arms apart,
lean down and see myself
wanting to shake him.

New Mother

for Merrill Strange

What you were is not what you are
now that your daughter is born.

You were, I thought, a beauty in time.
Why else run so much? Those x miles a day—
early morning, again in the evening
after biking home four miles from teaching school,
clocking your speed so carefully,
as if, the more you ran, the less time it would use up,
and growing fitness could gain on time
till it stopped passing,
and the finish line would never arrive.

Then you were big with her
and were told not to run anymore,
to turn your strength inward.
So you walked the same course every day.
I'd see you striding along,
throwing back your head as you arched your back
to hold up the belly going before,
swinging your rounding hips and taking your time
as the young runners passed by
with their stick figures.
Let them find the finish line!

The baby's here;
time hasn't stopped, it's started over.

Your husband, who watched you
push yourself inside out,
tells me never again
could he not respect a woman.

What you are,
a riper beauty, in her own time,
grows out of what you were.

THE ONE WHO GOES FINDS LIFE

Carson and Hilary start a support group
for infertile couples. Neither husband
goes to the meetings. Todd tells Hilary
"I don't want to talk it over with Rixey,"
and Rixey doesn't want to talk about adoption
or think about donor insemination.
Todd gives up on the Clomid Hilary's taking
when lo, it works. On a trip to England
they conceive. Meanwhile, Carson dreams
there's a baby in the next room:
she dreads getting up to find it dead,
but when Hilary goes in, the baby is fine.
Carson believes we're everyone in our dreams
and asks Rixey to pray for a dream of his own.

CAESARIAN

My little corporal, a transplanted kidney,
soldiers on, clears toxins at normal rates
from my cavern of male torso.
Untimely ripped from my sister indeed,
except she planned this parenthood
and will not have to die for my life.
"It's what I could show my kids about love."
She doubles over her ache *post partum,*
charged with the shorted nerve ends
of an amputee. "All mothers . . . feel that some."
And like all mothers when offspring grow away,
she can only hope that what I've learned
is to take care of myself, for love.

Radix Malorum

Christmas is a-comin',
The New Yorker's gettin' fat.
Please to put a penny
In the Chase Manhat.
If you haven't got a penny
Then a Visa Card'll do.
If you haven't got a Visa Card
Then Who are you?

The Eye of the Heart in the Mouth

*The eye of the head comprehendeth not. . . . In the
matter of comprehending God, the eye of the heart
has been bestowed by God.*

The Qur'an

If I, in the moment of clapping
my hand to my mouth, could fantasize
some rogue militia capitalist
recruiting a zombie McVeigh
to hijack a Saudi airliner
and crash it into Mecca
at the height of the *hajj*,
then I might stare Revenge
in its snake-framed face
and spew this sudden stone in my throat,
or squirm to swallow it down.

But once I've gone there, soreness rushes in
to open the clenched fist of insane logic,
that we might see, by grace,
how far from the black boxes
of demon-seized American planes
are the flowing feet of pilgrims
seven times circling the *Ka'ba*
and the hearts in hand all over the world
that bow and bow each day
and bow and bow and bow
to that still, small Eye of God.

23 September 2001

THE WIDENING GYRE

For poetry makes nothing happen.
—W. H. Auden, "In Memory of W. B. Yeats"

1. Coole Park, 1965

The rampage of the summer trees
Prospers over the crumbling house;
The tense lake trembles silent beneath
The portent of a lowering sky;
Toward the water my mother and I
Brave the bold reign of the breeze.

She sees this house beyond worst fears
Pursued to dust by only the years.
Of fifty-nine there are left two swans
With gray-faced young—no clamoring sound
Of soaring wings hushed weary now, downed
By rainstorms of restless careers.

She wonders at death's swift wage.
"So soon smothered the song-lived demesne
You might have remembered—and I feel old."
The orchard trees at Coole lie waste.
Of swallowed fruit a lingering taste
Declaims upon a barren page.

The storm will strike and the house shudder cold;
The swelling lake will encroach on the shore.
In seeming forage for gray-faced whimpers,
The old swans hide their heads in the water.
Mother know, growing old, that your daughter
Loses no orchard, being born old.

2. A Cold Eye on Life, on Death

If only you were only you
and not my mother. Then I could still rage
at your tantrum once against my sister's
donating me a perfect-match kidney
at the risk, you feared, of her own children.

You'd rather let me die, I heard you say,
as a harried bitch
must choose amongst her litter,
but I never could quote you on that
because you offered me life again—
your own old kidney instead,
though doctors decreed
that even the right cadaver's
would do better. So,
you could blame them.
And now, on down the road,
my sister's hale, still giving,
her strong daughters are off to college;
I'm still kickin' and you,
with your old bones crumbling—
you still want to choose:
no more surgery, right into hospice
with that second hip unmended.
Soon you will plead for me
to let you die
only you.
                    Woman, pass by!

THINK NO ELEPHANTS

In Sunday school
I dreaded leprosy.
Fixated, in high school,
on curatorial displays
(pictures of elephantiasis—
Africans trundling their balls
like pumpkins in a wheelbarrow),
I'd try to imagine dancing.

Now they grow between us,
still-born ones: your fibroid tumor
(white lobes big as five months gone
but never kicked, just clung to
and strangled your womb, which had to be
delivered itself);

and still not born: my swollen kidneys
(failing, nephrectomable).

Nights, we nestle in a fetal curl,
either inside the other—
a couple expecting
and not even trying
not to think about elephants.

MIRROR, MIRANDA
Moods and Tenses in the New Middle Age

How old would you be if you didn't know
how old you are?
                                        —Satchel Paige

I. Subjunctive: *"If I were only I . . ."*

The only common uses of the subjunctive mood in modern English are
to express a condition contrary to fact and to express a doubt or wish.
          —Warriner's English Composition and Grammar, p. 578

Free Fall

                         Mirror, mirror, we do not see
ourselves as others see us—
                         not on our own walls

where still we strut and suck it up,
turning and turning, sucking it in

for the vignettes
of each one's
                    private mental salon.
                                        No,

it's the chance glass
of a streetscape,
                    side glance passing

a teller's window
that bares my proportions—
                         belly swagging,

stick arms swinging my shopping bags
as daydream mind warms up

to put shots Olympic, toss javelins
through five linked rings,

throw hammers beyond horizons—
                              or simply to fall off
(inertia's grace)
                    in a swan dive
                                  down

from the highwire
of constantly risked absurdity

down
        down
                down beside
                        down
on banks and banks of TV screens

in the window-wall of the next shop,
where all my neighbor selves
                              be stretched against the sky,

one cloud in orbit
                a nano-eon between
the *Challenger* roaring up,
                        Columbia sifting down

and destined for a miry soup
(blood mud
            and melted bones)

to fill that impression
the end of a free fall
                    makes.

II. Imperative or Interrogative: *"You* will *laugh with me?"*

The imperative mood expresses a direct command or request. Usually a German asking a favor will simply inflect the command upward at the end. Down in our bedrock selves, where the roots of language are reaching, we are all Germans.

Love Me *Still*

> *Too fuckin' busy and* vice versa.
> —Attributed to Dorothy Parker

For this stanza, call my wife
Miranda, she who must be wondered at
for many reasons.
          Now,

Miranda, before I ask you to jump again
in the empty air of more time together,
look back with me on past moods and tenses
and let us sing a mirthful, self-forgiving dirge.

No need to paint you like Dilsey,
with "myriad and sunken face"
and "a paunch almost dropsical"—

gravity enough in our younger years
when I competed mostly with myself
and did not run enough laps of your races,
barely dreamt your desires.

There was no simple past, no perfect,

so Dorothy now
          (oh yes, you *were* born,
circumstantially, in Kansas),

let us get busy with *vice versa.*

III. Past Perfect: *"The railroad had ridden upon others before us . . ."*

The past perfect tense, formed with had, *is used to express action completed in the past before some other past action or event.*
—*Warriner's*, p. 569

Trains in Virginia and Elsewhere

1. My Primal Scenes

Trains in Virginia were always so near—
right down Main Street in the middle of Ashland
at a courtly pace between the front lawns,
dogwood tops at passengers' eye level.
Tracks frayed out onto piers at Newport News,
where engines uncoupled (in front of everyone,
not off in the yards) and backed up sidings
to shove their cars on the ferry to Norfolk.
A boy felt tiny beside a throbbing cab,
blasted with gouts of brake steam
as I reached out to touch the monster's hide
and the engineer glanced down from on high.
    Up country, too. Returning once to Richmond,
our engine sprang loose on the straightaway
through White Oak Swamp, and spurted miles ahead
till the driver jumped at the straining speedometer.
Back down the line, the jilted coaches
coasted to a stop. We piled out onto the ballast, toeing stones
till the engine grew into view again,
abashed, back-pedaling hard as it could.
In the space of that time,
the virgin swamp crept closer, full of cries.
Honeysuckle and kudzu, chirring and rustling,
snuggled right up to the roadbed.

70

2. Your Diana Childhood

In Philadelphia, that walled-off city
where you debuted, fathers channeled trains
onto the Main Line, a four-track highway
limiting access to a girl like you.
No crossings at grade, tunnel or footbridge
at every station, strict No Trespass signs
against walking onto the roadbed.
The Broadway Limited, hugging an inside track,
would almost suck the windows out
of standing locals. Your daddy's big yard
backed up to the tracks, but a steep bank
shut out the eyesore, muffled the noise.
A perfect range for your archery set,
but if you overshot, forget the arrows.
      When your period came, you called it your train,
soaking up the general dread of lateness.
We joked about having to keep it all in
whenever we got close to being prone,
and I whispered another secret fear
from my border days in Alexandria:
over the river at Union Station,
where big city trains down from the North
first land on the South, I'd wait for another
to coast in too fast like the one in '52
that surged onto the passenger concourse
and plunged, meteoric, to the floor below.
      I'd squint with the eyes of that frantic engineer,
who died in the wreck with his hand on the air-brake.

3. Our Bacchanal

Carson and Rixey, loving and playing hard
in Charlottesville.

We'd shortcut along the C & O tracks
through back yards of the best fraternities.
Fresh legends ballooned
of lovers passed out on the tracks,
crushed like old pennies. Outgoing freights revved up
to yank their mile of gondolas
up the westward incline toward the mountains,
rattling the brothers' every window.
Incoming trains were quiet, coasting.
One night the FFV—Fast Flying Virginian,
crack all-Pullman, strictly first class—
whisked around the curve at Beta Bridge
and blasted us with the horn at fifty yards.
Hand in hand, we leapt to the side, whooping
and laughing panic. Inside that wall of noise
by the rushing cars, toeing stones again
in the roadbed, clinging to you,
I knew I'd been that driver before.

IV. Imperfect: *"I used to helm this tangent line of love . . ."*

Whereas the perfect tense was used to indicate a single act *in past time, the imperfect portrayed an action as* going on, repeated, *or* habitual *in past time.*
—Frederick M. Wheelock, *Latin: An Introductory Course,* p. 71

De Finibus Bonarum et Malorum

They exchanged the nautical technicalities.
—John Crowe Ransom

1

Your mother loved with sharper Yankee sense,
And cleated many a tack before she'd knot
Her mooring to the common recompense
Of ship and port. She implicates, you plot
A similar course beyond my thirsting shoal;

Race in the prudent channel, and come about
By circling all the buoys close. Too droll,
Their woo and whistling, only to mean "Look out!"
　　Under commission you sail, and I am land
By force of imagery, touched on your charts
As rocky hazard to commerce of hearts.
But hold your course; conceit of my smooth sand
Defines your port, where buoys clamor
In awe of still shallower glamor.

2

For I would helm my tangent line of love
Great circle sailing past this polar freeze,
That our meridian compass all degrees
And we escape these latitudes of Jove.
　　But East hates West, these days?—that's foreign news.
Blue cordons here blockade the love I'd choose.

3

Awash in silt at the neap-tide of love,
My galley is charged with forgetfulness
Of groundswelling passion, the wash that drove
You back to port and me to becalmed distress.
　　My hulk, in this most need of reckless salvage,
Will not break up till you disturb the sea,
Nor ever sink, except thou dredg'st me free.

V. Present Perfect: *"She has waited upon the Lord"*

The present perfect tense, formed with have *or* has, *is used to express action occurring at no definite time in the past, or occurring in the past and continuing into the present.*
—*Warriner's*, p. 569

My Wife on the Gospel Side

1. At Seminary
She's always seen far
through her own eyes darkly,
pounded out questions all day long,
swept webs from the farthest crannies
to let the Empress Truth go naked.
I know her heart still pounding
will plague the devil himself for answers.

2. Jill in the Pulpit
She finds the taste of brass in her mouth,
knows she could smell her doubts
if she lifted her arms in the Spirit.

Her knees knock, her hands shake;
she fears her voice may tremble, too,
but we don't see a thing.

We only see her hearing the Word,
see her believing,

and never have to feel
what the vision costs.

3. Strait is the Gate
Good little girl brings gospel news,
Real rage in her trembling hand
At God, who seems to pick and choose
Which prayers to understand.

VI. Gerundive: *"Hoc est miranda mihi"*

*The gerundive, which is another name for the future passive participle,
is used primarily in the passive periphrastic conjugation. To quote the
reassuring pedagogic words of Frederic M. Wheelock:*
   *Despite its horrendous name the passive periphrastic is simply the
gerundive with* sum *in any form required by the sentence. The passive
periphrastic expresses obligation or necessity:* Hoc est faciendum mihi,
This is to be done by me; Haec Caesari facienda erant, *These things were
to be done by Caesar. Instead of the ablative of agent, the dative of agent is
used with the passive periphrastic, as illustrated by* mihi *and* Caesari *above"*
                    —Latin: An Introductory Course, p. 112

Admired Miranda

*Indeed the top of admiration, worth
What's dearest to the world!*
                    —The Tempest

1

Gerundives, turning verbs to nouns,
actions into being—
what art does to life—
are recognized by their *–n*dings:
hence, *memorandum*, what must be remembered,
and *agenda*, what ought to be acted upon.
This grammatical posture
                    staggers
                              too close
to the graceless impersonal passive (in which
the former direct object is made the subject
and the agent is left unstated—Caesar was praised
Caesar laudatum est—and which my English teacher
excoriated in our 9ᵗʰ-grade papers).

But if, in meditation, object disappears
into subject, the passive voice
just may express "annihilation" of self,
the dissolution of separate being

75

in pure and uncreated light.
That mystical surrender liberates.
When we exercise our free will to choose necessity,
we can *want* to be instruments
of the will of God, "whose service is perfect freedom."

2

By virtue of Wheelock's little lesson
on the dative as opposed to ablative of agent,
the passive results of gerundive acts
(which the subject merely receives)
are gained not "by means of" his or her doing
but rather "to or for" that person,
as with an indirect object,
the beneficiary or butt of the action,
depending on how you regard Fate.

And if, in poetry, under the dispensation
of Sister Gerundive, agent and sufferer are one,
subject and object the same—
Miranda est admiranda mihi
"must be admired (to or for) me"—
why, lovers can become right now
the indirect objects of their own future actions!
What better syntax for the rewards of faith?

Now, as a Southerner, I must admit
gerundive could be
the ultimate masculine gaze,
still objectifying the female,
still making her subject *to*
while pretending to make her the
subject *of.*
        But if the gaze be mutual,
it can burn away all ground between
two butterflies casting their eyes
     from opposite perches
both in the same direction.

VII. Future Conditional: *"No pain, no gain"*

Ut sit mens sana in corpore sano.
—Juvenal

*The future conditional is not strictly a mood or tense but an
adverbial relation between an action and a future result:
If I work out, I will lose weight and be strong.*

*Juvenal's maxim (In order that there may be a healthy mind
in a healthy body) is carved on the pediment of the old gym
at my school. It uses the good old adverbial ut-clause of
purpose, which in Latin takes the subjunctive (prompting
cynics to suspect that our purposes are just wishes or
doubts, or contrary to fact).*

*But if we show faith and loyalty, can we not turn a doubtful
outcome into a reliable salvation?*

Falling Together

What, then, is the future condition of love
in our nights remaining?

For you, Miranda,
forty years my wife gerundive—

for you, babe, and me
it's step aerobics
Nordic track trekking
Nautilus lift and press—
rites together rites
together
rep rep reps together

ut sit ut sit ut sit
in corpore
till outta body
in *compostellas* of the *mens sana*

we're mirror acting,
no glass but each other

finger tips and palm to palm
                                nose brush nose,

our being One
               each other's whole agenda,

not blinking but *drink* to me
                         only with

To me? Ah, drink me
               in! Yes,

    swill me in swirl me up

          up into
      up
up

                     dervish whirl
                          semahane
                                 Sufi
      FAN-A!

falling down
           falling down
                fall into

Beloved's eye,
       heiros gamos,

wrapped in our very own
               Shiva arms,
self-embracing
       each other

           Shakti Shakti Shakti

VIII. Future Perfect: *"We shall have loved . . ."*

The future perfect tense is used to express action which will be completed in the future before some other future action or event.

—*Warriner's*, p. 569

Dancing Away

As when th' heart says, sighing to be approv'd,
'O could I love!' and stops, God writeth 'Lov'd.'
—George Herbert

Having tried trains and boats
in our pasts perfect and imperfect,

let us now dance away
and learn to fly.

Up now, ancient of Wisdom,
walkabout
          and about must go

to songline drumming
                in
cosmic ground

cupping our ears
          for
music of the spheres

freeing up *una anima*
to bloodtrack the moon
               by

splashed blazes of ochre
along her beaten way

of the many *Sophias*—
          Artemis Isis Astarte

Devi Hagar Diana
　　　　　　　　the Virgin　Magdalene—

every *Sapientia*
　　　　　single mother to suckling science,
tasted sap of knowledge.

　　　　　　　　And we, Miranda,

because you've tended horses—
Dudley Charlie Horse Scooter—

　　　　　　　　　　native dancers all

because you've served each one
you've led,
　　　　　mucking grooming and

guiding with gentlest aids,
with barest touch
　　　　　of spur or crop—

when we ride out
from Pegasus' history,

sphinx-head mounted Centaurian,
charioteer astride
　　　　　and wings on every foot,

through mire and main,
　　　　　　　　our six wings grafted
seraphically
　　　　　to hooves and ankles,

new mandala sealed
　　　　　hermetically
in our joint
　　　　　imaginations

Mirror, mirror, mirandala—

Presto!
　　　　we shall have been unmired,
still falling still getting up
　　　　　　　　to dance away, intact
　　　　and broken open.

TIME'S END, WILL RESTORE

Bought this house, woke up
with a baby older than we are.
It grows on us,
new moss on sitting stones.
We stir and stretch
to keep our crusts from closing over.
We'll scrape and prime as we can,
curing the shed skins,
boiling them down in the
very hearth. We bought this farm
to wake again.

Maison Natale (almost)
408 South Lee Street, Alexandria, Virginia, where WPE was
brought home from the hospital on his second day in 1947
in post-War America, in an old bureau drawer for a cradle.

Snapshot by WPE, during Garden Week, 2004.

AUTHOR'S APPRECIATION

First I would like to thank the Patrons, Donors, and Friends whose remarkable generosity has made the publication of this book possible.

My thanks to many members of The Word Works for their help in bringing this book to the light, from the receptive reading of Miles David Moore, Steven B. Rogers, Ann Rayburn, and Jim Beall to the careful proofreading of Mike Davis and Judith McCombs and the graceful book design of Janice Olson. Karren Alenier, Miles Moore, and Nancy White offered truly devoted editorial guidance, with many insightful suggestions that pushed these poems toward realizing their potential, both individually and collectively.

Many thanks to Claudia Emerson and Henry Taylor for their graciously agreeing to read the manuscript. I owe much to earlier teachers, including Peggy Bevington, Fred Bornhauser, A. E. Claeyssens, John Coleman, Stanley Plumly, Susan Tichy, and especially Peter Klappert, who has left his indelible mark on my work invisibly, by teaching me what to leave out. Over the years Jane Schapiro, Naomi Thiers, and Jonathan Vaile have given abundantly of their friendship and wise attention to help bring these poems into a presentable shape. More recently I have enjoyed the added support of Romola Dharmaraj, Judith Freeman, Kathi Morrison-Taylor, and Katherine Smith.

Thanks of long standing to many colleagues and students at Woodberry Forest School and Episcopal High School, especially Pilar Andrus, Richard Barnhart, Anne Bingham, Ted Blain, Anne Carver, Leslie Hiers Chadwick, Elizabeth Crosby, Bob and Beth Eckert, Jim Ellington, Will Frazier, Michelle Gil-Montero, Joe and Joey Halm, Bill Hannum, Eric Heginbotham, Kathy Howe, Fraser Hubbard, Paul Huber, Thom and Ruth Hummel, Rich Johnson, Charlie Lovett, Peter Meister, Whit Morgan, Mason New, Hilary and Tom Parker, Charlie Porter, Forrest Pritchard, Molly Pugh, Riker Purcell, John Reimers, Bob and Johanna Smethurst, John Walker, Ned Walter, and Baobao Zhang, and most recently to Tim Rogers and Kathleen Lawton-Trask for help with proofreading.

I am grateful to David Douglas for help with digital images and inspiring discussions of the challenges of artistic form, to Will Mebane for the author photograph and a warm reminder of the role of grace in creation, to Steven White for being there to take the cover photo, to Rene Aranzamendez for critical help with permissions to reprint epigraphs, and to Dody Vehr for providing a writing house at Fiddler's Green. I will long remember ardent conversations with some great discerners of poetry: Champ Atlee, Peter Barrett, Chris and Caroline Brown, Andy Cadot, Peter Coy, Dave Dowling, Paul Erb, Brad Gioia, Leslie Adkins Gunnels, Billy Holliday, Bob James, Buzz Kellogg, Bob Lesman, Mel McKay, Tim Pickering, Greg Potter, Jeff Price, Charley Symes, Phil Terrie, Maria Tjelveit, Peter Way, and Joan and Jeff Whitehead.

I have taken to heart many life lessons gained together with true soulmates: Elizabeth Allinson, Emma Gail Allinson, Page Allinson IV, Page and Betsy Allinson, Mary Shipley Allinson, Chloe Andrus, Marc and Sheila Andrus, Claude and Tally Bandy, Lew and Mary Baylor, Tim and Lizzie Berner, Mariann and Paul Budde, Tim and Merrill Carrington, Betsy and Henry Chapin, Alan and Jennifer Dowding, George and Ellen Galland, Joseph and Julia Gunnels, Peter, Rawley, and Winston Gunnels, Grant Harmon, Annabel Hughes, Linda Kaufman and Liane Rozell, Tom McCusker, Harriet Moore, Angus Randolph, Jill and John Scarrott, Darrell Smith, Merrill and Phillip Strange, Clarke and Nancy Tucker, and the Colleague Group (The Reverends Willie Allen-Faiella, Zack Fleetwood, Doug McCaleb, Jo Ann Murphy, and Daniel Robayo).

I offer this book with thanks to all of my immediate and extended family: in memory of my father; in tribute to my three sisters, Isota, Maria, and Katherine, who have given me life in ways both tangible and intangible; in hope and expectation for my nieces and nephew, Caitlin and Anna Barrett and Melissa and Gregory Potter; and in honor of the remarkable creative life of my mother, Isota Tucker Epes, who lived just long enough to rejoice in the news that *Nothing Happened* would finally happen. Lastly, I dedicate this book to my wife, Gail Allinson Epes, ever the "onlie begetter" of my best thoughts and truest feelings. She gave the final touch and grace note to this collection by sitting down with me to sift and settle the order of the poems.

—William Perry Epes

ABOUT THE HILARY THAM CAPITAL COLLECTION

The Hilary Tham Capital Collection (HTCC) is an imprint of The Word Works featuring juried selections from poets who volunteer to assist The Word Works in its mission to promote contemporary poetry. In 2011, a prominent poet with no affiliation to The Word Works will judge manuscripts and select the next HTCC book.

In 1989, Hilary Tham was the first author published in the Capital Collection imprint. In 1994, when she became Word Works Editor-in-Chief, she revitalized the imprint, which had produced only two titles. By June 2005, Ms. Tham had paved the way for publication of thirteen additional Capital Collection titles.

The following individuals and organizations have contributed to the HTCC to make this book possible:

PATRONS: Page and Betsy Allinson • Charlotte Dudley Cleghorn • Isota Epes and Gregory Potter • Hattie Gruber • Harriet and Billy Holliday • Anne and Leonard Long • Miles Moore • Philip and Caroline Squair • Jonathan Vaile.

DONORS: Mrs. H. M. Cadot • Sandy and Meade Cadot • Merrill and Tim Carrington • Oona Coy • Bob and Beth Eckert • Maria Epes • Mr. and Mrs. F. Robertson Hershey • Paul Huber • Myong-Hee Kim • Dr. and Mrs. Joseph Lawton • Chuck and Jean Brown Leonard • Richard Lyons • Julie I. Malone • Frank and Leila Martin • Judith McCombs • Pamela McMullin • Kathi Morrison-Taylor • Rob and Diane Pierce • Cornelius D. Scully • *Sow's Ear Poetry Review* • John Stillwell • Julie T. Vehr • Steven White • Bruce and Claudia Williams • Eleanor Williams • Bud and Kate Wright.

FRIENDS: Lee S. Ainslie • Richard Barnhart • Anne Carver • Christopher Conlon • Marie Louise and Simon Davidson • Shelley deButts • Viviana R. Davila • Episcopal High School Book Club • George and Ellen Galland • Robert E. James • Peter Klappert • Steve and Kirke Lisk • Maggie and Vollie Melson • Whit Morgan • Dave Phillips • Molly Pugh • Ann Rayburn • Stephanie and John Reimers • Kitty Riordan • Elinor Scully • Sarah Stone • Elizabeth Vorlicek • The Rev. Fred S. Wandall.

Thanks to our generous anonymous contributors.

ABOUT THE WORD WORKS

The Word Works, a nonprofit literary organization, publishes contemporary poetry in collectors' editions. Since 1981, the organization has sponsored the Washington Prize, a $1,500 award to an American poet. Monthly, The Word Works presents free literary programs in the Chevy Chase, MD, Café Muse series, and each summer, free poetry programs are held at the historic Joaquin Miller Cabin in Washington, DC's Rock Creek Park. Annually, two high school students debut in the Miller Cabin Series as winners of the Jacklyn Potter Young Poets Competition.

Since 1974, Word Works programs have included: "In the Shadow of the Capitol," a symposium and archival project on the African-American intellectual community in segregated Washington, DC; the Gunston Arts Center Poetry Series (Ai, Carolyn Forché, and Stanley Kunitz, among others); the Poet-Editor panel discussions at the Writer's Center (John Hollander, Maurice English, Anthony Hecht, Josephine Jacobsen, and others); and Master Class workshops (Agha Shahid Ali, Thomas Lux, Marilyn Nelson).

In 2010, The Word Works will have published 70 titles, including work from such authors as Deirdra Baldwin, J.H. Beall, Christopher Bursk, John Pauker, Edward Weismiller, and Mac Wellman. Currently, The Word Works publishes books and occasional anthologies under three imprints: the Washington Prize, the Hilary Tham Capital Collection, and International Editions. Information on Toad Hall Editions, a publishing division of The Word Works, can be seen at ToadHallMedia.com.

Grants to The Word Works have been awarded by the National Endowment for the Arts, National Endowment for the Humanities, DC Commission on the Arts & Humanities, Witter Bynner Foundation, Writer's Center, Bell Atlantic, Batir Foundation, and others, including many generous private patrons.

The Word Works has established an archive of artistic and administrative materials in the Washington Writing Archive housed in the George Washington University Gelman Library.

The Word Works   PO Box 42164   Washington, DC 20015

editor@wordworksdc.com   www.wordworksdc.com

Other Word Works Books

Hilary Tham Capital Collection
Mel Belin, *Flesh That Was Chrysalis*
Doris Brody, *Judging the Distance*
Sarah Browning, *Whiskey in the Garden of Eden*
Christopher Conlon, *Gilbert and Garbo in Love*
                Mary Falls: Requiem for Mrs. Surratt
Donna Denizé, *Broken Like Job*
James Hopkins, *Eight Pale Women*
Brandon Johnson, *Love's Skin*
Judith McCombs, *The Habit of Fire*
Kathi Morrison-Taylor, *By the Nest*
Miles David Moore, *The Bears of Paris*
                Rollercoaster
Maria Terrone, *The Bodies We Were Loaned*
Hilary Tham, *Bad Names for Women*
                Counting
Jonathan Vaile, *Blue Cowboy*
Rosemary Winslow, *Green Bodies*

Washington Prize-winning books
Nathalie F. Anderson, *Following Fred Astaire* (1998)
Michael Atkinson, *One Hundred Children Waiting for a Train* (2001)
Carrie Bennett, *biography of water* (2004)
Peter Blair, *Last Heat* (1999)
Richard Carr, *Ace* (2008)
Ann Rae Jonas, *A Diamond Is Hard But Not Tough* (1997)
Frannie Lindsay, *Mayweed* (2009)
Richard Lyons, *Fleur Carnivore* (2005)
Fred Marchant, *Tipping Point* (1993)
Ron Mohring, *Survivable World* (2003)
Jay Rogoff, *The Cutoff* (1994)
Prartho Sereno, *Call from Paris* (2007)
Enid Shomer, *Stalking the Florida Panther* (1985)
John Surowiecki, *The Hat City after Men Stopped Wearing Hats* (2006)
Miles Waggener, *Phoenix Suites* (2002)

International Editions

Yoko Danno & James C. Hopkins, *The Blue Door*

Moshe Dor, Barbara Goldberg, Giora Leshem, eds., *The Stones Remember*

Myong-Hee Kim, *Crow's Eye View: The Infamy of Lee Sang, Korean Poet*

Vladimir Levchev, *Black Book of the Endangered Species*

Additional Titles

Karren L. Alenier, Hilary Tham, Miles David Moore, eds., *Winners: A Retrospective of the Washington Prize*

Jacklyn Potter, Dwaine Rieves, Gary Stein, eds. *Cabin Fever: Poets at Joaquin Miller's Cabin*

Robert Sargent, *Aspects of a Southern Story*
A Woman From Memphis

Breinigsville, PA USA
25 April 2010
236748BV00002B/4/P